SEEDS

text and pictures by Ken Robbins

ATHENEUM BOOKS FOR YOUNG READERS
New York • London • Toronto • Sydney

sprouting wheatberries

What you need to know about seeds is that they sprout. There's energy in every seed, and inside each seed another plant that wants to grow.

These are wheatberries—seeds that I kept moist in a jar. Just a few days later, look what happened.

Seeds come in
many, many sizes
and shapes.

Every different sort of plant
has a different sort of seed.

Though every seed has the power to make a new plant, not every seed will do it.

SWEET PEAS
ROYAL MIXED COLORS
(LARGER BLOSSOMS, LONGER STEMS)
$1.49
ANNUAL HEIGHT
3-4 FEET
NET WT. 4G

To grow, each seed must move (or be moved) to a place where everything is exactly right—where there's just enough moisture, just enough light, and just enough space for the new plant to grow.

milkweed
seeds

Other seeds wind up by
chance in places where they
are able to grow.

cherries

From the seeds
that farmers sow,
in the spring and
summer come
wonderful fruits—
delicious, sweet
plums and cherries,
peaches, apricots,
and many others.

plums

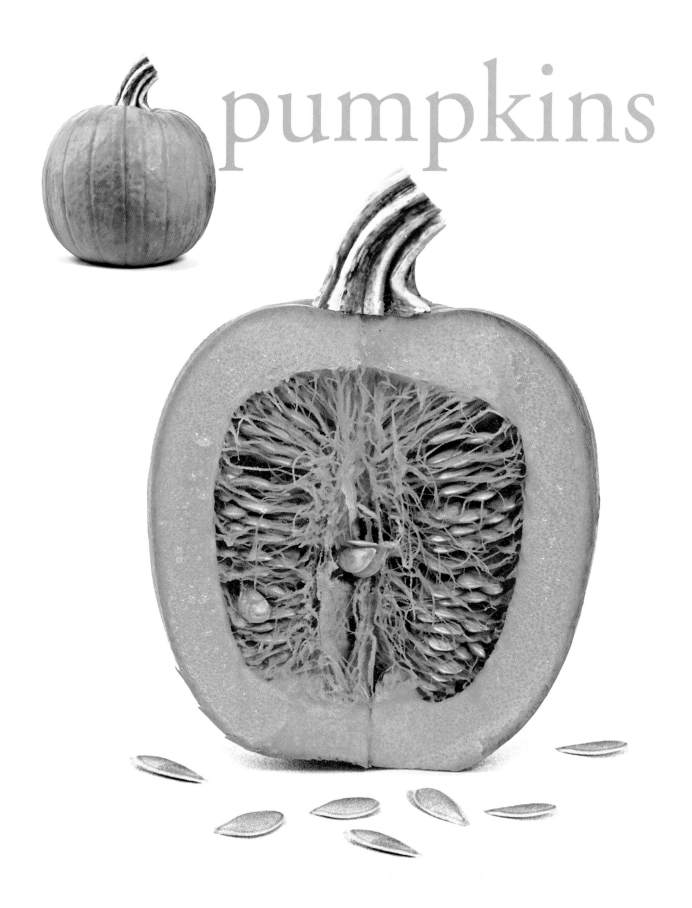

pumpkins

melons

If you ever had a watermelon
in the late summer, or carved
a jack-o'-lantern from a pumpkin
in the fall, or cut a slice of juicy red
tomato with a knife, then you've seen fruits
that have not just one, but many seeds inside.

wheat

When you eat a sandwich, consider this: The bread is not much more than the seeds of a grass called wheat, ground up into flour and mixed with some water and a little bit of yeast.

corn

Corn is another kind of grass. The seeds are formed in clusters. The clusters, of course, are known as ears. The seeds are known as kernels.

If you go for a walk in the woods in the fall, and you happen to pass some sticktight plants, the chances are you'll come back with a bunch of their seeds on the cuffs of your pants and stuck to the tops of your socks.

sticktights

berries

Raspberries and blackberries are clusters of sweet and juicy beads that birds (and people) love to taste. Even when they're eaten, the seeds remain alive, and eventually they drop to the ground—often many miles away by then—and the seeds take root.

acorns and oaks

If you stand under a big oak tree in the fall, you'll see thousands of acorns all over the ground. The acorns, of course, are the seeds of the tree.

Squirrels eat them, but they often bury them first, saving them up for another day.

Sometimes, though, the squirrel forgets where it put them. The squirrel's mistake becomes a brand-new oak tree.

dandelions

When the yellow
flower of the dandelion is
dry, what's left are the seeds in a
fluffy white ball. If there's a wind (or
if you blow on the seeds), they float on the
breeze and settle when and where they will.

maples

You see the seeds of the maple tree everywhere in the middle of spring. They have wings called samaras that make them flutter in the breeze as they fall from the trees like tiny helicopters.

impatiens

The impatiens is a
pretty plant whose
flower produces a tiny
pod. When the pod is
ripe, at the slightest
touch the seeds go flying.

lotus

The lotus grows not in the ground, but in the water. Its flowers make a fruit of sorts, and the fruit produces seeds. The seeds dry up, fall off, and are carried away downstream.

coconuts

The coconut palm grows in tropical zones, often right by the sea. When its seeds are ripe, they fall off and some of them land in the surf. They catch a ride on the currents and waves, and sooner or later they wash up on another shore. There, another palm tree may grow.

avocados

The seed of an avocado is called a pit, and with it you can have some fun. Try this: Stick some toothpicks in its side and set it, with the flat end down, in a glass or jar that is mostly filled with water.

In a week or two (or maybe more) the pit will start to crack and split. Some roots will stick out from the bottom. A stem and leaves will grow from the top. It's now an avocado plant.

For Rebecca Kuperschmid

Thanks to Paige St. John and Arya Berg of Bayberry Nursery
for their substantial expertise and patient explanations; to
Lauren Jarrett, helpful as ever; and to Diana Duff.

Atheneum Books for Young Readers
An imprint of Simon & Schuster Children's Publishing Division
1230 Avenue of the Americas, New York, New York 10020
Copyright © 2005 by Ken Robbins
All rights reserved, including the right of reproduction in whole or in part in any form.
Book design by Alex Ferrari
The text for this book is set in Adobe Garamond.
Manufactured in China

8 10 9
CIP data for this book is available from the Library of Congress.
ISBN 978-0-689-85041-7

1010 SCP